the little book of smart

paul jackson

smart * smart * smart
new
edition!
smart

D0756542

www.veloce.co.uk

First published in December 2007 by Veloce Publishing Limited, 33 Trinity Street, Dorchester DT1 1TT, England. Fax 01305 268864/e-mail info@veloce.co.uk/web www.veloce.co.uk or www.velocebooks.com
This new edition published March 2009. ISBN: 978-1-845842-72-7/UPC: 6-36847-04272-1
© Paul Jackson and Veloce Publishing 2007 & 2009. All rights reserved. With the exception of quoting brief passages for the purpose of review, no part of this publication may be recorded, reproduced or transmitted by any means, including photocopying, without the written permission of Veloce Publishing Ltd. Throughout this book logos, model names and designations, etc, have been used for the purposes of identification, illustration and decoration. Such names are the property of the trademark holder as this is not an official publication.
Readers with ideas for automotive books, or books on other transport or related hobby subjects, are invited to write to the editorial director of Veloce Publishing at the above address.
British Library Cataloguing in Publication Data - A catalogue record for this book is available from the British Library. Typesetting, design and page make-up all by Veloce Publishing Ltd on Apple Mac.
Printed in India by Replika Press.

the little book of smart

paul jackson

smart • smart • smart • smart • smart

new edition!

VELOCE PUBLISHING
THE PUBLISHER OF FINE AUTOMOTIVE BOOKS

contents

introduction & acknowledgements

introduction

From the launch of the very first city-coupé back in 1998, to the vital American debut of the latest fortwo a decade later, the smart brand enjoyed impressive progress through its first ten years. Although the company went through some low points during that time, it has emerged as a strong, specialist brand producing exactly the right range of cars at exactly the right time.

The future of smart now looks assured, aided by the fortwo's impressive economy, low emissions, and all-round quality. But smart has learned a lot over the last decade, and has plans to develop the fortwo further and to introduce it to new markets to ensure its continued success.

You can read about it all here, this second edition of *the little book of smart* providing an opportunity to bring the smart story bang up-to-date. This is a company with a fascinating past and a genuinely exciting future. Enjoy!

acknowledgements

Grateful thanks are due to all the members of the smart press office in Britain for their help in researching this book, as well as Rod Grainger at Veloce Publishing for his assistance and encouragement. Also, thank you to Paul Guinness for supplying much of the photography used throughout the book.

Paul Jackson

chapter 1

smart move

With smart being such a well-known car brand these days, it's easy to forget just how young a company this really is. In fact, it wasn't until July 1998 that production of the two-seater smart city-coupé first began, paving the way for some impressive successes – and more than a few disasters – during the subsequent years. But how did it all begin?

At the start of the 1990s, it was an open secret that Mercedes-Benz was keen to expand its product line-up. The company certainly wasn't short of executive models, but the success of the 'small' 190 series (launched in 1983 and a major hit for the marque) showed that the expertise was there to open up the brand to a new, less affluent audience.

What the company needed was an even smaller model that could take the Mercedes brand into new territory. The company took a look at the success of the Volkswagen Golf, for example, and realised it wouldn't mind a slice of that particular action. And Mercedes-Benz

did eventually join the Golf set, launching its revolutionary A-class to a shocked public at the end of 1997 before it went on sale throughout most of Europe in the spring of '98. What a drastic change of direction that was.

Yet even while the A-class was just a glint in Mercedes' corporate eye, management at the company began thinking the almost unthinkable. The forthcoming A-class was going to be small, but was there potential for the firm to develop an even tinier model?

In January 1993 that Mercedes-Benz officially launched a feasibility study on the development of a city car. But what exactly was its thinking then? Quite simply, it wanted to revolutionise urban transport, and predicted that, by the end of the 90s, the market for small cars would be very different.

joint venture

The chance to create something almost

When the smart city-coupé took a bow in 1998, it marked a major departure for both Mercedes-Benz and the small-car market in general. This brand new, Mercedes-owned company had created something unique – but would the car-buying public of Europe and beyond take to the concept?

It was certainly a brave move. With a rear-mounted, three-cylinder engine, a two-seater layout and a bodyshell that derived its strength from the revolutionary tridion safety cell, the all-new smart city-coupé was unconventional in the extreme. At long last, small-car buyers were offered something genuinely different. (Courtesy smart)

outrageously different moved up a gear when, on March 4th 1994, a press conference announced to the world a planned joint venture between Mercedes-Benz and what was then SMH – known today as The Swatch Group Ltd. It was exactly the kind of deal that Mercedes had been looking for; but why did it feel the need to jump into bed with another company in the first place?

Swatch had already been carrying out research into the feasibility of entering the motoring market when the joint venture was announced. The Swiss watchmaker, famous for its trendy design-led products, could see a future for a Swatch-badged urban two-seater that set new standards in both funky design and up-to-the-minute technology. And, happily, this wasn't dissimilar to the early conclusion that Mercedes' engineers and developers had come to; just as the A-class was to be different from anything else at its price, so a sub-A-class Mercedes had to be unique within the city car class.

Just one month after this joint venture was announced, a new company was created by Swatch and Mercedes-Benz, registered at Biel in Switzerland and going by the name of Micro Compact Car AG. By the end of 1994, a location had been chosen for what was to be the new company's state-of-the-art production facility: Hambach in France. Things were now moving at a rapid pace.

Indeed, by September 1995, even before construction of the new factory had got under way, Micro Compact Car AG had its first concept vehicle built and ready for reaction. It was, in essence, an early example of what was to become the MCC smart city-coupé.

The prototype followed the various ideas that Swatch had been working on prior to the link-up with Mercedes-Benz. The engine was situated at the rear; the cabin was a spacious two-seater; and the structure comprised a steel 'skeleton' with plastic panels attached. Where it differed though, was in its surprisingly conventional engine; Mercedes decreed that a three-cylinder petrol unit should be used in place of the hybrid idea that Swatch had been working on.

rapid progress

Undeterred, Micro Compact Car AG ploughed on with its development, making use of Mercedes' skilful engineers and Swatch's understanding of successful design and marketing. By the end of 1995, the foundation stone for the company's new Hambach factory was being laid; there was no going back now.

It was at this time too, that the smart name itself first came into being. Micro Compact Car AG began referring to smart in various announcements, which – as history went on to prove – meant the name Swatch wasn't to

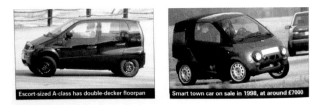

Escort-sized A-class has double-decker floorpan | Smart town car on sale in 1998, at around £7000

By the mid-1990s, the world's motoring press was full of stories of Mercedes' future plans; in particular, coming up with spy shots and artists' impressions of the forthcoming A-class and, of course, the all-new smart.

'Escort-sized A-class has double-decker floorpan', boasted one news story, followed by 'Smart town car on sale in 1998, at around £7000'. And while that UK feature was right in much of its detail, the photograph of the heavily-disguised smart prototype managed to make the newcomer look clumsy and goggle-eyed. Readers must have wondered what kind of miniature monstrosity was actually coming to the marketplace ...

(Courtesy Paul Guinness)

appear on the vehicle after all. What many had assumed would be one of the newcomer's biggest marketing ploys – use of the renowned Swatch branding – wasn't on the agenda any more.

With the benefit of hindsight, of course, this was indeed a sound move. Just a few months after the MCC smart city-coupé finally went into production, Micro Compact Car AG was the subject of a 100 per cent takeover by what was then Daimler-Benz AG. The Swatch involvement was officially at an end, and MCC and smart were now wholly part of the Mercedes family.

Why did Swatch pull out of the project at the last moment? There was talk that

management at the Swiss watchmaker was disappointed with some aspects of the car – not least its conventional powerplant. It's also possible that, with Swatch originally intending the car to be a cut-price product aimed at young buyers, it felt the car had moved too far upmarket. The city-coupé, when launched, was far more expensive than Swatch had ever intended.

But that didn't matter. So radical were certain aspects of the exciting new smart city-coupé, it was guaranteed to catch the imagination of small-car buyers worldwide. Or rather, that's what was hoped after such a major investment ...

Just one of the features that made the all-new smart city-coupé unique was its tridion safety cell, a powder-coated steel structure that provided the new smart with its integral strength, and the skeleton from which its thermoplastic 'skin' would be hung. This allowed smart to offer a wide range of different coloured body panels, enabling customers to personalise their smarts quickly and easily.

Thanks largely to this clever tridion design, the smart city-coupé soon found itself receiving praise in various European crash tests, with EuroNCAP applauding the newcomer for being 'very strong and stiff in frontal impact'. (Courtesy smart)

The first eagerly-awaited smarts rolled off the line in Hambach on July 1st 1998. But what about the production process itself? With a vehicle as unique as the smart city-coupé, you'd be right to assume that production processes would be slightly different from the norm. For a start, smart took environmental issues very seriously, way beyond any legal demands of the industry. 'The ecological requirements are laid down in a whole string of specifications', explained the company, going on to say: 'and for smart GmbH it is essential that its system partners take these requirements just as seriously.' (Courtesy smart)

smart was particularly proud of the ecological benefits of its tridion design: "The painting technique used for the tridion safety cell is an innovation in the automobile industry worldwide, thus contributing to a maximum in environmental compatibility.

"For the first time in the automobile industry, powder-coating is used for the entire vehicle bodywork. Some of the ecological advantages of our powder-coating process are no water consumption, no waste water, no paint sludge and no solvent emissions. The overspray is also reused in an internal materials circuit."

For environmentally-conscious buyers, this was all excellent news. (Courtesy smart)

While the Hambach factory in France was the official production base for the smart city-coupé, the company's engine manufacturing was carried out in Berlin, at a new facility created by Mercedes-Benz.

Manufacture of the innovative three-cylinder smart engine got under way in 1997, a good few months before the city-coupé's anticipated launch of early the following year, enabling smart's engineers to ensure the new powerplant was fully developed. This, after all, was the smallest turbocharged engine to be fitted in a European city car, and customers had to trust its long term durability if the smart concept was to succeed at all. (Courtesy smart)

It was unusual for a car manufacturer to feature production processes so much in pre-launch publicity, but with smart it was a clever ploy. In an age when consumers were becoming increasingly environmentally aware, it was an effective way of gaining some very positive publicity.

It succeeded in presenting the smart city-coupé as the car that even the most ecologically-minded consumers could buy with a clear conscience; and, just like the design of the actual vehicle, this was a rather useful unique selling point. The pre-launch publicity was well under way! (Courtesy smart)

The city-coupé was originally due to be launched in early '98, but disaster struck when it was discovered that handling wasn't as stable at the limit as its designers had anticipated. In fact, when pushed into certain cornering tests at speed, the diminutive smart was likely to topple over!

This was a huge embarrassment to all involved, and inevitably meant a redesign and delay of the official launch, but this was preferable to an unmodified car going on sale and being damned by the press. Before any buyers were allowed to get behind the wheel, the city-coupé had to be absolutely right. (Courtesy smart)

Part of the redesign included narrowing the front wheels and widening the rears, resulting in bigger back wheelarches than the original stylists had intended – although the overall effect of this was very pleasing. This was accompanied by a suspension upgrade, retaining the original front leaf springs and the coil-sprung de Dion rear setup, but firmed to ensure less body roll. At this early stage, smarts were also being equipped with what the company called its TRUST suspension design, though this would later be upgraded to TRUST-PLUS – a relatively sophisticated piece of kit complete with electronic traction and stability control. (Courtesy smart)

Poor publicity and a delayed launch date was bad news for smart, and even before the city-coupé went on sale its production targets were being revised to save any further embarrassment. What had originally been estimated as a 200,000-unit market throughout Europe was soon downscaled to sales of 100,000 smarts for 1999 – the model's first full year on sale. In fact, at the start of '99, production was stopped completely for a whole two weeks in an effort to reduce stocks and allow demand to catch up with supply. There couldn't have been worse news for all those involved ... (Courtesy Paul Guinness)

The eventual launch of the city-coupé (several months behind schedule) meant some good news at last for smart, although it remained to be seen whether small-car buyers would take to such a radical concept. Would the car's two-seater layout, for example, attract customers or deter them? Research showed that most of the cars bought as urban runabouts rarely carried more than one passenger, so maybe smart was on to a winner after all. The fun and funky design of the car's interior certainly helped it win friends, particularly among those younger buyers bored by conventional economy cars. (Courtesy smart)

By the late 1990s, car safety was a major marketing tool, and smart knew that one of the questions that would regularly be asked of its diminutive new city-coupé was just how safe it would be in the event of an accident.

Independent tests carried out by organisations like EuroNCAP and DEKRA confirmed that the smart was one of the sturdiest and safest city cars on the road, a tribute to its innovative tridion safety cell concept. Indeed, in this controlled collision carried out by DEKRA, the smart survived in a dramatically healthier state than the less fortunate Fiat Seicento.

(Courtesy smart)

19

The new smart city-coupé was like no other offering in the city car class. While rival companies like Fiat (with the Cinquecento) and Ford (with the Ka) had gone for a combination of modern styling and utterly conventional mechanicals, the all-new smart was revolutionary in every aspect of its design.

Its design and build processes hadn't come cheap, though, and the city-coupé couldn't be offered at the same kind of bargain-basement price as some of its natural rivals. In fact, by city car standards, the smart was a premium-priced product, albeit justified by its hi-tech specification and unique concept. (Courtesy smart)

Three trim levels of the new city-coupé were initially made available, known as smart & pure, smart & pulse and smart & passion. All shared the same 599cc, three-cylinder motor, though in two different states of tune.

Power for the entry-level pure totalled a mere 45bhp, while at the top of the performance tree sat the pulse and passion models with a healthier 54bhp (developed at 5250rpm). Top speed was electronically limited to 84mph, with 0-60mph in a fairly unspectacular 17.5 seconds – although, in fairness, any city-coupé always felt more rapid than that in day-to-day use. (Courtesy smart)

Transmission on all models was smart's newly developed, six-speed sequential design, comprising three forward gears operated through two final drive ratios. It could be used in fully automatic mode (called Softouch by smart), or as a semi-auto with automatic clutch and sequential gearchanges.

Driven as a fully automatic, the early smart city-coupé never seemed quite as happy. Many testers criticised the set-up for continually hunting for the right gear, and being very hesitant about selecting the ideal one; it could make for jerky and frustrating progress, leading many owners to stick with the far-more-fun sequential setting at all times. (Courtesy smart)

As October 1998 arrived, those customers in Belgium, Germany, France, Italy, Luxemburg, Austria, Switzerland, Spain and The Netherlands who'd been placing orders since July that year finally began taking delivery of their new smarts. Their response was crucial; the early success of smart lay in the hands of the car-buying public of nine European countries. Happily, the reaction was generally enthusiastic and smart began establishing itself as the new name in chic urban transport. As sales began to rise, the future looked much rosier – despite the decision by Swatch to withdraw from the project altogether within weeks of the city-coupé's launch. (Courtesy Paul Guinness)

chapter 2

the early days

It was hoped that once deliveries of the first smart city-coupés got under way, the controversy over those earlier handling difficulties would start to fade. It's true that both consumers and the motoring press have frustratingly long memories at times; but it's equally true that, with a product as distinct and different as the smart, onlookers would be more interested in the looks, design and driving appeal of the car than in its earlier pre-launch difficulties.

Even so, early sales predictions had to be drastically downscaled in order to prevent major embarrassment at the end of the year. In fact, in December 1999, smart had quite a celebration when the 100,000th city-coupé rolled off the production line in Hambach, coinciding with another major announcement: the launch of the diesel-powered smart cdi.

It was easy for industry pundits to question the need for a diesel version of such a small car, but smart had done its research and reckoned sales of diesel-powered economy cars were going to escalate at an unprecedented rate in the early 21st century.

off with its top!

For those buyers who demanded the most fun rather than the best fuel consumption from their smart, the next big news came in March 2000 with the eagerly awaited announcement of the smart cabrio.

The idea behind it was simple, as were the engineering changes. Because of the city-coupé's unusual design and construction method, using the tridion safety cell to give the car its strength and rigidity, the idea of removing the roof was remarkably straightforward. The rear section of tridion acted as an in-built roll bar, while the plastic roof and rear window areas were replaced with an electrically-operated folding fabric roof.

Fortunately for the car-buying public, smart

did an excellent job of developing the smart cabrio. Even better news was the fact that the exciting new smart cabrio was also the least expensive proper convertible on sale in Europe, despite costing up to 30 per cent more than the equivalent city-coupé (depending on which trim level the buyer opted for). smart had a trendy new product on its hands that, for once, wasn't criticised for being overpriced; things were definitely looking up.

Even so, smart couldn't afford to become complacent, and both the city-coupé and the cabrio found themselves on the receiving end of improvements and enhancements on an annual basis, helping to transform the city-coupé in particular into a far more user-friendly and sophisticated product than those earlier examples.

onward and upward

Comparing the specification of a 2003-model city-coupé with one from four years earlier, for example, really brings this home. The most significant change was the enlargement of the three-cylinder petrol engine, up from 599cc to 698cc thanks to a bigger bore and longer stroke. This resulted in the entry-level pure derivative having a power output of 50bhp, with the passion boosted to 61bhp. And because the engine wasn't having to work as hard as before (as well as being aided by an improved electronic management system), official figures showed an average of up to 60mpg with careful driving.

Then there was the smart's transmission, one of the most criticised areas in any road test of an early-model city-coupé. In fully automatic mode it was slow and ponderous, and as a semi-auto sequential set-up it was equally jerky. smart took this to heart, and in 2002 equipped the city-coupé with a drastically modified transmission.

When used in fully automatic mode, the new setup was much quicker and smoother than before; it even boasted a good old-fashioned kickdown feature, something that was previously sadly missing and a major improvement when it came to safer overtaking and extra power when it was needed.

Handling-wise, those later city-coupés were also a real improvement over their predecessors. Despite the early production smarts being generally considered safe and competent after the pre-production stability scares, smart was determined to improve things still further. And that's why, by 2002, all new city-coupés came equipped with Electronic Stability Program (ESP), a feature originally developed for the forthcoming new roadster range but which proved just as effective in transforming the city-coupé.

All these improvements went a long way towards broadening the appeal of the smart

As time went by, the city-coupé's growing list of improvements transformed it into a far more likeable, more powerful and easier to drive urban runabout. By the end of 1999, the 100,000th city-coupé had been built, and the following year saw increased sales for the company – aided by two major model introductions.

Meanwhile, the standard city-coupé's appeal continued to grow, its reputation as a chic and trendy city car ensuring plenty of appeal on Europe's most congested streets. Sales in Italy were particularly strong, while UK imports got under way in 2000 – albeit in left-hand drive guise only, as shown here. (Courtesy smart)

line-up, with extra sophistication, power and refinement finally provided. And such changes weren't lost on the motoring press either, with praiseworthy road tests appearing throughout Europe. The smart city-coupé had managed to grow into an impressively sophisticated and highly developed product, without losing any of its unique character or charm. Increased sales levels in most of its markets were the proof that smart was finally on the road to success.

One of the great advantages of the smart city-coupé for motorists with a sense of individuality was the ease with which its body panels could be swapped for another complete set. Certainly a cheaper option than having a conventional car resprayed! This is how your average city-coupé looked with all outer body panels removed, ready for a new set to be screwed in place. While any smart dealer in Europe would be happy to order a complete set of panels and fit them for you, many owners preferred to do the job themselves. (Courtesy Paul Guinness)

Establishing new markets for the city-coupé was essential to the future success of smart. Reasonable sales throughout Britain of left-hand drive models during 2000 led to the launch of a right-hand drive version (pictured here) the following year. And by 2002 the city-coupé was also making inroads into Eastern Europe, with countries like Hungary, Slovakia and the Czech Republic receiving official smart imports.

Indeed, so determined was smart to ensure that the city-coupé and the company's forthcoming new models were destined for sales success, by 2004 the brand was being sold in no fewer than 35 countries worldwide. (Courtesy smart)

While standard city-coupé colours included lite white, phat red and jack black (complemented by a black or silver-coloured tridion safety cell), those who fancied something different could order panels in star blue metallic, bay grey metallic, river silver metallic, scratch black, numeric blue or stream green.

Choosing a colour scheme had never been so much fun! And even now, if you pay a visit to any smart owners' gathering anywhere in the world (particularly when there's a smart club involved), you'll see just how personalised these cars can become. (Courtesy Paul Guinness)

Announcement of the smart cdi for the 2000 model year introduced the world's smallest production diesel engine to the line-up, a 799cc common-rail, direct-injection, three-cylinder powerplant.

Developed from the existing smart engine, the diesel version needed its extra 200cc to keep power output at a reasonable level – in this case, 40bhp compared with the city-coupé pure's 45bhp.

Where the cdi really scored was in fuel consumption (up to 70mpg in daily use) and a CO_2 emissions rating of just 90g/km, an achievement that – in smart's own words – made the cdi "a real contribution to climate protection". (Courtesy Paul Guinness)

This was the smart that so many enthusiasts had been looking forward to. The eagerly-awaited smart cabrio finally took a bow in March 2000, and in most of the markets it entered was the least expensive convertible on sale. That alone should have been enough to guarantee sales success, but the cabrio's appeal was far greater than its sheer affordability.

With the electrically-operated fabric roof folded back, and the driver making full use of the newcomer's open-air fun appeal, the cabrio became one of the must-have fashion accessories of the new millennium – much to the delight of smart. (Courtesy smart)

Thanks to the city-coupé's tridion safety cell, transforming it into a genuine soft-top was possibly the easiest cabriolet 'conversion' ever carried out by a major manufacturer. Having said that, smart took time and money to ensure the design was spot-on from day one. The hood had to glide effortlessly, as well as be completely watertight when shut; noise levels had to be roughly in line with those of the hardtop city-coupé, and the whole car had to retain the feeling of quality and robustness that the city-coupé had already been praised for. The end result? Impressive by any standards. (Courtesy smart)

What smart needed for its new cabrio was a favourable press reaction. How would Europe's motoring journalists react once they got behind the wheel of this affordable new convertible? Happily, mostly the Press was suitably impressed. "This could be a red letter day for sun lovers", enthused Britain's *Auto Express* magazine after its testers had got their hands on a smart cabrio for the first time. It went on: "smart has delivered a different way of getting wind in your hair with a soft-top that can claim to be the cheapest new cabriolet currently available ..." (Courtesy smart)

To give the new smart cabrio an appearance as distinct as possible from the city-coupé, it was fitted with redesigned headlights – soon known as the 'peanut style' due to their unusual shape. This simple but effective modification succeeded in giving the fun little cabrio an identity all of its own.

Most buyers thought they looked great. And so did smart, it seems: by 2002, the 'peanut' headlamps were being fitted as standard, not just on cabrios but across the city-coupé range, too, all part of a mini facelift and a range of improvements carried out that year. (Courtesy smart)

The original decision not to sell smarts in the UK was revoked once British enthusiasts began buying examples provided by unofficial importers, with companies bringing over left-hand drive smarts and selling them at premium prices. And so it was that the first official UK smart imports went on sale through a couple of smart centres, and via the Internet in January 2000.

So good was the response that smart realised there would be an even bigger market if it tooled-up for right-hand drive production. The first right-hook city-coupés went on sale in the UK in October 2001. (Courtesy smart)

Manufacturing right-hand drive smarts for British consumption meant other potential markets were inevitably opening up for the city-coupé and cabrio. In fact, just about any country that employed right-hand drive could now be considered a potential export market for smart.

And so it was that the steadily improving and increasingly popular smart city-coupé was officially launched in Japan in November 2001, the first time ever that a non-Japanese car, with the tiny dimensions demanded by that country's tax-saving K-class light-vehicles sector, had been sold there. Yet another European car was about to become a Japanese cult. (Courtesy smart)

BRABUS had long been associated with go-faster Mercedes-Benz models, having built some superb high-powered saloons and sports cars over the years, all of them using Mercedes models as their basis. So it was only a matter of time before the company officially got to grips with creating more powerful smarts, culminating in the creation of smart-BRABUS GmbH in March 2002.

With ownership of the company split 50/50 between MCC smart GmbH (as it was still then known) and BRABUS GmbH, this was very much a joint venture. And the first priority was to take the city-coupé in a whole new direction. (Courtesy smart)

Official BRABUS versions of both the city-coupé and cabrio (shown here) went on sale, looking magnificent thanks to their BRABUS-designed body kits, and offering extra performance and handling thanks to the engineering changes that had gone on under the skin. The main point about those showroom-ready BRABUS models, though, was to demonstrate what was available from an exclusive new range of accessories and upgrades. Relatively few buyers would choose the mightily expensive full BRABUS package, but at least the ready-made BRABUS city-coupé provided a useful 'menu' from which buyers could choose whichever modifications they desired or could afford. (Courtesy smart)

Even without considering the huge range of BRABUS upgrades, smart owners were spoiled for choice when it came to accessories for their city-coupés and cabrios, with the official smart brochure of the time featuring a vast array of goodies.

From eye-catching new body panels to alloy wheels, and from bike racks to satellite navigation systems, smart had just about everything that any customer was likely to demand. Well, very nearly!

Europe's newest car brand was doing rather well by offering customers so much personalisation – and smart owners simply couldn't get enough of what was on offer!

(Courtesy Paul Guinness)

chapter 3

smart evolution

With its fortunes improving by the start of the 21st century, smart knew it had to keep both products and brand name at the forefront of the city car market. But while the city-coupé was being steadily improved and the new cabrio was selling well, what else could be done to draw even greater attention to this publicity-hungry manufacturer? The answer was finally revealed at the 71st Geneva Motor Show of February 2001.

It was known as the crossblade, an exciting concept car based around the smart cabrio. It took roofless motoring to a new extreme by also removing the cabrio's doors and windscreen, the latter replaced by a narrow transparent wind deflector. Strength was maintained thanks to the tridion safety cell which was kept intact; attached, though, were radically 'chiselled' body panels for a dramatic, futuristic look.

The crossblade concept wouldn't have looked out of place in a moon-based sci-fi film. And its radical appearance was further enhanced by gloss black body panels and tridion's titanium grey powder-coated finish. The combination looked mean, moody and more than a little mad!

The trick worked, because the world's newspapers and motoring magazines were full of images of this amazing concept car from smart. Surely, though, even such an adventurous company as smart wouldn't dare to put into production something so radical – would it?

major change

While all this was going on, the city-coupé was being steadily upgraded and improved, although it wasn't just the little smart's engine and transmission that came in for major enhancements. As the previous chapter mentioned, the smart range of 2002 onward also came complete with the company's new

Electronic Stability Program (ESP) facility. But what did this mean in reality – and how did it work?

Originally developed for the exciting new smart roadster range that was on the horizon, ESP was designed to replace the previous TRUST-PLUS driving control system (which itself had been very effective), taking the whole concept a stage further. By making use of selective brake intervention to stabilise the car when needed, ESP added Hill Start Assist, Brake Assist, ABS and Electronic Brake-force Distribution (EBD) to the mix. It was, quite simply, the most technologically advanced package of handling improvements ever seen in the city car class.

All of this helped to give the highly developed new-generation city-coupé a head start in what was becoming an increasingly competitive market. And a rather welcome knock-on effect of ESP's excellence was that smart could now soften the city-coupé's suspension settings, as well as introduce greater spring travel. This resulted in a vastly superior ride quality, something the original city-coupé had always been criticised for.

These latest models now felt better developed, more grown up and far more comfortable than ever before, whilst not losing any of their inherent fun appeal. It was a difficult balance to achieve, but smart did it admirably. Oh, and just in case these changes encouraged new owners to drive further in their smarts, the city-coupé now came complete with a larger fuel tank.

new name, new era

It was, however, one of the city-coupé's most important single features that ended up being replaced completely in 2003: its name. While city-coupé had proved an effective badge for five years, the start of a new era was just around the corner for smart, and the company decided that a new and more suitable model name was now needed.

These were exciting times for the company, with smart determined to expand rapidly and no longer rely on just one basic design for success. New roadster and roadster-coupé models were being launched in 2003; a four-seater forfour was planned for 2004; and an SUV by the name of formore was likely to take a bow in 2006, finally enabling smart to enter the all-important American market. Somehow, the name city-coupé just didn't sit neatly amongst this fresh, modern line-up.

The new name couldn't have been more logical. If a four-seater smart was going to be known as a forfour, the existing city-coupé could just as easily be re-branded as a fortwo. And that's exactly what happened. The fortwo coupé and fortwo cabrio had arrived.

It was quite right that the city-coupé should finally have a new name, as those latest versions were, in so many ways, brand new cars. In fact, the 2003 fortwo shared just 30 per cent of the components used in the 1998 city-coupé, according to smart. So, as the city-coupé faded away to be replaced by the fortwo, a new era was beginning for smart.

Changing the name from city-coupé to fortwo for smart's original offering was a logical move, given the company's future plans. With a four-seater hatchback under development going by the name of forfour, adopting the fortwo tag for the two-seater couldn't have been more apposite.

As it turned out, however, the all-new forfour was to be a sales flop, one of the factors that led smart to have a rethink about its future direction by 2005. But none of that was anticipated at the time of the fortwo's launch, prompting smart to boast of a four-model line-up being on sale within a few years. (Courtesy smart)

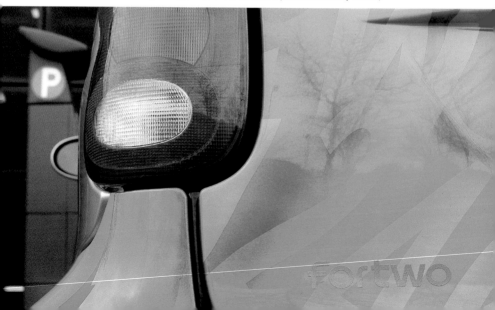

The adoption of a new name was appropriate for smart, as by 2003 just 30 per cent of the original city-coupé's components were still used in the fortwo. Uninformed onlookers may not have noticed most of the changes at first glance, but beneath the skin the fortwo was a very different machine altogether, thanks to such enhancements as an upgraded driving control system, improved suspension, and much more.

The baby smart had never looked so grown up, and Europe's motoring press responded with some favourable road test reports. (Courtesy Paul Guinness)

45

The smart fortwo was winning widespread acclaim for the sophistication of its design, while enthusiasts loved the steering wheel-mounted, paddle-type transmission controls that became an optional extra. Changing gear sequentially in a city car had never been so much fun!

Sales of the fortwo were on the rise, with Germany, France and Italy being particularly healthy markets for smart. The UK was also becoming increasingly important, aided by decent press reaction. Back in January 2003, Britain's *Auto Express* magazine said: "With progress like this, the smart brand looks set to go from strength to strength." (Courtesy Paul Guinness)

The creation of the fortwo line-up saw BRABUS' involvement in the smart brand continue, with official BRABUS versions of both the coupé and cabrio made available. And smart was rather proud of these latest versions: "The technical heart ... is a tuned 55kW (74bhp) standard engine. This engine is exclusive to the fortwo BRABUS equipment line and is not available as an option. It offers smart customers a sporty driving experience with maximum torque of 110Nm."

Top speed was increased to 94mph for easier cruising capabilities, while acceleration was aided by that new torque level. The end result? An impressive little driver's machine. (Courtesy smart)

With 74bhp developed at 5250rpm, any BRABUS fortwo offered useful – and very noticeable – extra power over the standard models. Engine capacity remained the same at 698cc, but the boost to both power and torque transformed the feel of the fortwo when ordered in BRABUS guise.

Magazines like *What Car?* (based in the UK) described the BRABUS' performance as "nippy rather than quick", recording a 0-60mph sprint time of 12.3 seconds in the process. In reality, though, the BRABUS always felt more rapid than that, adding to the all-round appeal of this hugely entertaining (if rather expensive) version. (Courtesy smart)

Thanks to the latest Electronic Stability Program (ESP), the BRABUS fortwo offered much-improved handling and roadholding, as smart explained: "ESP ensures that smart cars always follow the direction in which the driver steers, even at the stability limit of driving dynamics. In addition to closing the throttle valve and opening the clutch, ESP also offers brake intervention, acting on individual wheels. This ensures directional stability and road adhesion when accelerating, braking and coasting. Within physical limits, ESP ensures that during fast cornering cars neither push over the front axle (understeer) nor push outwards with the rear end (oversteer)." (Courtesy smart)

While the standard fortwo offered paddle-shift sequential gear changes as an optional extra, this steering wheel-mounted set-up came as standard on the BRABUS fortwo coupé and cabrio, adding hugely to the sporty feel and driver feedback of both models.

Elsewhere inside the BRABUS, buyers were treated to sports seats, aluminium trim, and other goodies, most of which could be ordered as BRABUS accessories from any smart centre if the customer preferred. For a car originally created as a hi-tech urban runabout, the fortwo could be made to look pretty exciting – inside and out. (Courtesy smart)

To say that the prototype smart crossblade created a storm at the Geneva Motor Show of 2001 wouldn't be an exaggeration. It generated enthusiastic headlines throughout the world, prompting the most obvious question of all: would smart ever have the courage to put the crossblade into production?

Of course it would. Twelve months later, again at Geneva, the production-ready smart crossblade was unveiled, and it was announced that a full 2000 examples would be produced in total. Fanatics who had enthused so much about the idea a year earlier could now get their hands on a crossblade. (Courtesy smart)

Taking a prototype from concept to production reality within a year of first showing it was a major achievement, a fact that wasn't lost on Andreas Renschler, chairman of the management board of smart at the time: "The fact that we have developed the smart crossblade within a year is further proof of the potential of our vehicle concept, and at the same time it is a further step towards extending our product range. After the almost euphoric reactions at last year's Automobilsalon in Geneva, we have decided to offer this car to our customers."

All smart needed now was 2000 buyers ... (Courtesy smart)

For anybody who assumed a crossblade could never be a practical proposition, smart released this tongue-in-cheek shot of a production version on its way to the golf club ... While production crossblades differed from the original prototype in minor styling details (such as front and rear wheelarch treatment), the concept behind the car remained unchanged. Here was a no-compromise funster for those who didn't demand such luxuries as a roof, doors – or even a proper windscreen.

There was nothing else on sale that could be called a genuine rival to the crossblade, so it's perhaps no surprise that smart had little trouble selling all 2000 examples.

(Courtesy smart)

The most famous crossblade buyer? None other than singer Robbie Williams, who took delivery of the first production crossblade in April 2002. He'd loved the concept from the moment he first saw it, and had been in discussion with smart ever since to ensure he had the very first of the 2000 produced.

On delivery of his crossblade, Robbie enthused: "Wow, I just love this car. It's innovative and unconventional, the two main qualities I look for in new projects." The fact that he and smart had already been involved in some joint publicity projects no doubt helped ...

(Courtesy smart)

With owners of larger motor caravans and recreational vehicles being known for their love of small cars, towing them behind their holiday vehicles and using them as daily transport once at the campsite, it was only a matter of time before a special trailer became available for hauling around the smart city-coupé and fortwo.

This happened when Britain's Bantam Trailers launched its unique 2.5-metre trailer, specially designed for carrying the smart. And it didn't take long for smart to recognise the usefulness of the trailer, which, by 2005, had become an official smart accessory available from smart centres throughout Europe. (Courtesy smart)

The many changes made to the smart fortwo began to pay off by 2004, with sales increasing at an impressive rate throughout Europe. But it was Britain that was proving one of smart's most impressive export successes.

In fact, March 2004 proved to be smart UK's most successful month to date, with sales up a massive 16.5 per cent on the company's previous best. Jerry Simpson, head of smart in the UK and Ireland at the time, said: "These excellent sales results mean that smart continues to be one of the fastest growing automotive brands in the UK market place." (Courtesy smart)

The smart fortwo cabrio continued where the city-cabrio had left off, with steadily increasing sales throughout Europe – particularly during the summer months. And in the UK – a country that (despite its unpredictable climate) traditionally enjoys more sales of convertibles and cabriolets than any other in Europe – it became especially popular.

By the summer of 2005, smart was celebrating five years of sales success in the UK, during which time a total of 45,000 officially-imported examples had found enthusiastic buyers. Despite original plans not to sell the smart range in Britain, it had become one of the company's most important export markets. (Courtesy smart)

57

By 2006, trials were being carried out on fully electric versions of the fortwo, showing how seriously smart was taking the idea of emissions-free motoring for the future. The UK was selected to run a market trial, with the new smart ev (electric vehicle) making its official debut at the British Motor Show that summer. Tests were under way by November of that year with selected corporate customers.

The smart ev boasted a 30kw output and a top speed of 70mph. It offered even better in-town performance than its petrol-powered stablemate, while also providing a range of up to 72 miles before needing recharging. (Courtesy smart)

How's this for a fortwo with a difference? It's the smart crosstown, a reinterpretation of the fortwo concept but with dramatically different styling and a hybrid drive power source. Although designed as a one-off concept vehicle, it showed the versatility of smart's tridion safety cell and the ease with which existing models could be restyled for different markets. This hybrid drive concept combined an electric motor (with an output of 23kw) and a 61bhp petrol engine, enabling a claimed reduction in fuel consumption of around 15 per cent over a standard fortwo. Was this a sign of smart's long term future direction? (Courtesy smart)

The last major activity before the launch of the brand new 2007 model fortwo came in
November '06, when smart unveiled the exclusive BRABUS edition red, a one-colour-only
limited edition that was instantly hailed as a future classic.
Powered by the same 74bhp BRABUS-tuned engine as before, the edition red had 'intense
red' body panels with matching tridion, front spoiler, side skirts and door mirrors, plus 16in
Monoblock VI alloy wheels. Inside were exclusive leather and Alcantara seats, dashboard
and door trims with contrasting red stitching, a three-spoke leather sports steering wheel,
air-conditioning, and special BRABUS aluminium pedals, gear knob and handbrake lever.
(Courtesy smart)

sporty smart

Aside from the limited edition crossblade, smart was still a single-model car manufacturer, with the fortwo coupé and cabrio models being hewn from essentially the same design. Frankly, that wasn't any use if smart was ever to be in with a chance of dramatically expanding its worldwide sales and eventually returning a profit for Mercedes.

There was nothing for it but to create new models, something that had always been part of smart's long term plans anyway. The logical move was to create a sporty smart, a car that would excite and tempt sports car fanatics around the globe – but particularly in the United States, where smart was banking on the success of its eventual launch there.

Not surprisingly, the most vital ingredient of any sporty smart had to be its fun appeal. Not just in a wind-in-your-hair kind of way, but fun in terms of sharp steering, tight handling, and an impressive power-to-weight ratio. It had to be a design of few excesses, yet instantly recognisable as a smart, even by those with little motoring knowledge.

It was a challenge, but by the time sneak photographs of concept smart roadsters began appearing in the world's press, it was obvious the stylists and designers were doing a fantastic job. And when visitors to Europe's various motor shows were first shown the smart roadster and roadster-coupé models in 2002, there was an air of genuine excitement. At last, it looked like one manufacturer had been brave enough to design a tiny, affordable and fun-to-drive sports car with more raw appeal than models like the Mazda MX-5.

eagerly-awaited

That the new smart roadster and roadster-coupé didn't go on sale in mainland Europe until April 2003 was an incredible frustration for thousands of potential buyers. But it was clever planning on the part of smart, which used the many months between the official unveiling and actual on-sale date to keep interest and excitement high. It also drew added attention to the smart brand throughout those months, which created a positive knock-on effect for the existing city cars.

Inevitably, both the new roadster and roadster-coupé made use of smart's now famous tridion safety cell – a feature unique to the brand. This provided the newcomers with all the benefits of a modular construction, which, in terms of build costs, ease of construction and any future restyles, was a positive boon for smart. The added customer benefits of a lightweight bodyshell, ease of accident repairs and, of course, unique two-tone appearance created by tridion couldn't be ignored either.

It wasn't just the tridion that gave the roadster and roadster-coupé their unique appearance, though. For a start, these were genuinely tiny sportsters – a full 548mm shorter and 65mm narrower than the MX-5 of the time. They also featured incredibly short overhangs, large wheels and pronounced body-contoured wheelarches which, when combined with the roadster's low ride height, gave a uniquely sporty and sexy appearance.

out on the road

Not unexpectedly, power for the new roadster and roadster-coupé came from an uprated version of smart's three-cylinder, six-valve turbocharged engine linked to the company's now famous six-speed sequential semi-automatic transmission. The engine itself was slightly larger than that found in earlier city-coupés, though its 698cc capacity soon became a feature of the renamed fortwo range. In roadster guise, though, output was a distinctly healthy 80bhp at 5250rpm, with 110Nm of torque at just 3000rpm (apart from a 61bhp entry-level model that was available in some markets).

At first glance, 80bhp from a two-seater sports car didn't sound a great deal – but here the opposite was the case. For a start, it was a truly impressive figure from just a 0.7-litre engine. And when fitted to a vehicle that weighed only 790kg, you suddenly ended up with a rather useful power-to-weight ratio of 101bhp per tonne. Now that was more like it!

The end result was a car which, despite offering what seemed like fairly unexciting on-paper performance figures, turned out to be one of the most entertaining driver's machines of its generation. The combination of an ultra-low driving position, oh-so-eager powerplant, rapid automatic gearchanges, and tenacious grip and handling meant that the roadster and roadster-coupé were massively engaging.

Even that wasn't enough for some buyers,

which inevitably meant BRABUS getting in on the action and offering its own uprated version for the roadster line-up. It had been a long time since fans of tiny sports cars had enjoyed so much choice!

Sadly, though, the good times weren't to last. Despite a promising start, production figures for the roadster and roadster coupé never did reach the levels where the models could become profitable and, as part of smart's major cost-cutting actions of 2005, the decision was made to cease production, with the final examples of the roadster and roadster-coupé finding buyers by early 2006. It was a sad day for sports car enthusiasts everywhere.

When it came to inspiration for its new sports car, smart unashamedly took a step back in time to perfect the concept. And even as the first prototypes were being unveiled, smart was making a feature of their nostalgic influences, claiming they "evoke memories of the compact and purist roadsters of the 1950s and 1960s. They reinterpret the purist roadster segment in form and design, coupled with today's demand for safety and comfort." The new smart roadster and roadster-coupé were intended to be the 21st century's equivalent of the MG Midget, Austin-Healey Sprite and Triumph Spitfire, it seemed. (Courtesy smart)

A sporty smart had to have two vital ingredients: it had to be fun (aided by sharp steering, tight handling, and an impressive power-to-weight ratio), and it had to be a design of few excesses, albeit one instantly recognisable as a smart.

It was a challenge, but by the time sneak photographs of concept smart roadsters and roadster-coupés started appearing in the world's press, it was obvious the designers were doing a fantastic job. When visitors to Europe's various motor shows were first shown the smart roadster and roadster-coupé models in 2002, there was an air of real excitement.

(Courtesy smart)

Real achievement could only be claimed if smart's sporting offerings were as fun to drive as their much-hyped pre-launch publicity had claimed. An aspect of the public seeing a new model long before it was available was that expectations continued to rise throughout the long wait. If those first buyers of April 2003 weren't to be disappointed, the new roadster range had to be good to drive. Damn good.

Happily, it was. As well as fulfilling smart's original objective of a basic sportster with a 1960s vibe, the newcomer was also actually a very sophisticated piece of kit.

(Courtesy smart)

The main difference between the roadster and the roadster-coupé was obviously the latter's all-glass fastback design – which gave the added bonus of a touch more luggage space. But which of these sporty smarts actually looked the best?

It was all down to personal preference, though you couldn't help admiring what smart had achieved with one basic design and a spot of creativity. There's an argument that the roadster looked more 'raw', more sporting even; but somehow the roadster-coupé's proportions were so perfect, it was this version that many buyers ended up choosing.

(Courtesy smart)

The smart roadster and roadster-coupé certainly weren't lacking when it came to creature comforts and on-board goodies. Standard equipment for the roadster in most markets included an electric soft-top, six-spoke, 15in alloy wheels, electric windows, electric power steering, CD player, and a leather-covered steering wheel and gear knob.

These machines may have been reinterpretations of those raw sportsters of the 1960s, but their generous levels of standard equipment ensured there was no hardship involved for those on board. In fact, considering their minuscule dimensions and nostalgia-inducing propaganda, these were surprisingly sophisticated little funsters. (Courtesy smart)

While the roadster and roadster-coupé generally boasted an output of 80bhp from a three-cylinder turbocharged motor, for many markets a 61bhp derivative was also available, offering a cut-price route to sporty smart ownership.

Opting for the 61bhp model (which also had less equipment, including – horror of horrors – steel wheels as standard) meant an inevitable saving on the list price. But, just as crucially, it also meant a reduction in insurance premiums, a crucial factor for many of the younger motorists at which the roadster line-up was aimed. It was a clever way of broadening smart's sporty new customer base. (Courtesy smart)

At first glance, 80bhp from a two-seater sports car didn't sound a great deal, but it was an impressive figure from a 0.7-litre engine. And when fitted to a vehicle that weighed just 790kg, you suddenly ended up with a rather useful power-to-weight ratio of 101bhp per tonne. How did smart keep the weight so low? Largely thanks to that tridion safety cell, which weighed a mere 192kg despite its incredible in-built strength and rigidity – both factors contributing to the roadster's impressive lack of scuttle shake, a major problem with some conventional sports cars. (Courtesy smart)

The first thing you noticed about the roadster as you climbed aboard was just how low down you were. The seating position was incredibly low-slung, particularly when compared with models like the Mazda MX-5.

The second thing you noticed was how smart's designers had carried over so many styling cues from the fortwo. The ignition key still slotted in just behind the gearstick; the chunky steering wheel was essentially the same; and the dashboard was very smartesque in style, particularly the two cowled pods ahead of the driver containing all the major instrumentation. It was all rather clever – and neat. (Courtesy smart)

The 80bhp roadster always felt faster than its official figures (109mph, with 60mph from rest in 10.9 seconds) might suggest. Get that 698cc motor working hard and the turbo spinning merrily, and you'd find yourself impressed by just how quickly the sporting smart pulled away from the line.

Despite this, driving a roadster at its limit was a drama-free experience. So effective was its Electronic Stability Program, it was difficult to upset the car's poise and agility, and the whole experience was putting the biggest grin on your face you'd had in a long time ...

(Courtesy smart)

When BRABUS decided to get in on the smart roadster action, it was obvious that something rather special would be the end result. The BRABUS roadster and roadster-coupé soon became permanent members of the official smart line-up in almost every market. BRABUS provided an exciting boost to performance thanks to various modifications, including a new turbocharger, an upgraded cooling system, and a revamped engine management chip. The result was 101bhp, which equated to more than 20 per cent extra power than a standard roadster – with performance to match. All impressive stuff. (Courtesy smart)

The BRABUS roadster and roadster-coupé also came with 17in alloy wheels, a special BRABUS radiator grille, side skirts and body-coloured spoilers. Things had changed inside, too, with aluminium and leather detailing giving a more exclusive look to what was already a pretty funky design.

Out on the road, other modifications made themselves known. BRABUS had carried out upgrades to the standard roadster's suspension which, when combined with the enormous new tyres, gave an incredible amount of grip – although some testers of the time preferred the feel of the standard roadster's wheel and tyre combination. (Courtesy smart)

The launch of the BRABUS roadster range wasn't the first time those tuning experts had got their hands on the sportiest smart. In fact, in the roadster's production debut year of 2003, they came up with the completely outrageous roadster-coupé V6 bi-turbo – just ten of which were produced to show exactly how far the little smart could be developed.

The bi-turbo V6 boasted two of the standard model's three-cylinder engines joined together to create a 1396cc twin-turbo V6. Power output was an astonishing 170bhp, with torque levels of up to 220Nm – both remarkable achievements from a 1.4-litre lump.

(Courtesy smart)

"Powered by Mercedes-Benz" boasted the bi-turbo V6's engine plaque, giving few clues as to this rare creation's astonishing performance potential. In reality, this meant a top speed of 137mph, passing the all-important 62mph mark in just six seconds.

With so few bi-turbo V6 models created, smart enthusiasts assumed they'd never get the chance to see one 'in the flesh'. But smart had other plans and, during 2003, arranged for the BRABUS bi-turbo V6 to take part in various smart events throughout Europe – including Britain's London to Brighton smart rally, organised by thesmartclub. The publicity it generated was invaluable. (Courtesy smart)

Right: Orders had been flooding in for the roadster since its unveiling in the autumn of 2002, and by the time deliveries started in mainland Europe in April '03 the future looked bright. In fact, during the remaining eight months of 2003, smart claimed it would be happy if the new sportster achieved sales of 8000 – but by the end of the year, no fewer than 20,200 examples had been built.

Still, it wasn't enough. Sales were high, but smart was making no profit from the roadster line-up. With the forfour selling poorly, the decision was taken in 2005 to discontinue the forfour and roadster ranges. (Courtesy smart)

By the time the new hatchback forfour model had arrived on the scene (see Appendix 1), the smart family had grown to its largest ever size – comprising the fortwo coupé and cabrio, the crossblade, the new forfour and, of course, the roadster and roadster-coupé models.

All smart had to do now was sit back and watch as each of its unique product lines took its own individual market by storm. Except, of course, that's not quite how it happened, with sales of the forfour in particular failing to live up to expectations. Worrying times were just around the corner. (Courtesy smart)

The premature ending of roadster and roadster-coupé production was a bitter blow to sports car enthusiasts everywhere, as well as fans of the smart brand in general.

To mark the end of production, a UK-only special edition of the roadster and roadster-coupé, known as the 'finale edition', was announced in April 2006, featuring 17in alloys and – on the roadster version – speed silver body panels with contrasting black tridion. With front and rear grilles in the same body colour, the car looked superb and was soon a sell-out. Surely this is one smart roadster destined for classic status in the not-too-distant future? (Courtesy smart)

chapter 5

fun and frolics

Any car that breaks design barriers and creates an entirely new market for itself is, by definition, going to appeal to individualists. This was particularly true of the original smart city-coupé; anybody who liked blending into the background would never buy such a unique machine. However, no matter how successful the city-coupé and its successor, the fortwo, were, it was inevitable that many owners would want to make their car that little bit more special. They loved the individuality of the standard cars – but why stop there? Happily, the design and construction of even the earliest smarts made this fantastically easy compared with most other small cars; it was only a matter of time before a whole new industry was catering purely for smart owners who wanted to be different.

change of hue

The beauty of any smart's tridion-based design

was that the plastic body panels attached to it have always been easily removable and replaceable – which means that if you get fed up with the panel colour of your car, you can invest in a full replacement set in another colour. And options are not just confined to colours either, as smart centres worldwide have always been able to supply body panels featuring a whole range of different designs and styles. You want to treat your fortwo to bright blue panels covered in a numeric logo design? No problem. You fancy driving round with a tartan finish on your smart? Hey, they're happy to help.

But why restrict yourself to the replacement body panels and paintwork designs offered by your official smart centre? For many owners, such a choice has never been enough. They don't just want their cars to be different, they want them to be positively unique. And that's why many enthusiasts have their own livery, decals, vinyl and designs applied to their cars, with end results ranging from the bizarre to the fantastic. From national flags to fruit, corporate logos to seascapes, the opportunities are limitless ...

a people thing

Not surprisingly, any car that attracts buyers with a sense of adventure is also going to encourage an active social scene – and that's why smart owners and enthusiasts have been having such a great time ever since the marque was first created, aided by large numbers of unofficial smart clubs throughout the world.

Most of these clubs offer members an active scene and plenty of opportunity to get together and enjoy themselves – so whichever club you belong to, you should find plenty happening for you to take part in. The most famous, however, has to be Britain's London to Brighton smart run, organised by that country's thesmartclub every year – and it's one of the world's must-see smart extravaganzas, renowned for attracting huge numbers of smart owners from throughout Europe.

Can you think of another new car brand that attracts this much fanaticism, this much affection, this much enthusiasm, and this much club activity? smart owners know how to have a good time; and they certainly know how to get the most out of their ownership.

smart's reputation for creativity and innovation broke new ground in 2003 when the company announced the 'smart individual' line-up – a range of special graphics available to city-coupé and fortwo owners. With a choice of ten different images printed on heavy-duty vinyl, which was then wrapped and stuck on to the car's body panels ... well, the end result was startling, to say the least!

And the options available? How about zebra stripes, cheetah spots, great white shark, London skyline, red tomatoes, tartan, Houses of Parliament, green lemonade bubbles, sheepdog or superhero? Something for everyone there, we reckon ... (Courtesy smart)

For those smart owners who want their cars to have a bit more attitude, there have always been smart specialists offering a good choice of spoilers, side skirts and full body kits to make any example that touch more sporting. And macho.

One of Europe's biggest suppliers of such kits is the UK's smarts-R-us, a company that offers a great range of merchandise – including its own body kits. You can buy individual items or complete kits, depending on your personal preference. Either way, though, it's a superb and relatively simple way of transforming an economical city car into something a little more 'street' ... (Courtesy Paul Guinness)

Changing your fortwo's original body panels for something more interesting has never been particularly difficult. Although your nearest smart centre will be happy to do the work, many owners see it as more of a weekend DIY task.

So, what do you fancy from the official smart line-up? A popular choice is numeric blue, shown here – an eye-catching design that helps give any fortwo coupé or cabrio a freshen-up. But if this doesn't appeal, you could always give scratch black or stream green a try. The choice is yours. (Courtesy smart)

While the BRABUS versions of the smart fortwo and roadster ranges have always been popular with those enthusiasts who wanted something genuinely different (albeit potentially pricey), it's the company's individual accessories that have particularly appealed to existing smart owners.

You'll find a good range of BRABUS-branded accessories and upgrades available for most smart models, and any smart centre will provide you with the latest prices and specifications of whatever it is you're interested in. From aesthetic improvements to engine and power upgrades, there's almost certainly a BRABUS solution available. (Courtesy smart)

Owning a smart wouldn't be the same without the social scene provided by scores of clubs worldwide, many of which enjoy fantastic support from owners, enthusiasts and trade alike. But it's Britain's annual London to Brighton smart run that is one of the most amazing smart events you're likely to see anywhere.

Whichever model they own, smart owners from throughout Europe (and beyond) take part in this extravaganza each year, helping to spread the word about smart ownership and enthusiasm – and having huge amounts of fun in the process. Check out www.thesmartclub. co.uk for further details. (Courtesy smart)

Ever fancied going rallying in a smart? Britain's Emma Saxby and Miles Moorhouse did in 2002, when they drove a smart city-coupé 4000 miles from London to Athens as part of that year's World Cup Rally.

The car travelled through an impressive twelve countries in twelve days, tackling a route that took in France, Belgium, Germany, Austria, Slovenia, Croatia, Bosnia, Montenegro and Albania. Emma enjoyed proving the durability of the little smart: "You usually see smart cars driving along city streets, so I thought it would be a great opportunity to put one through its paces on some of the worst roads in Europe." (Courtesy smart)

How's this for something different? Cruising along in your very own smart fortwo, it was possible to give yourself the beach body you always dreamt of, thanks to this set of images available for your smart's bolt-on panels. The only trouble was, the illusion quickly disappeared as you stepped from your smart and onlookers saw the reality of a less than perfect physique. Ah well ...

Male and female versions were available, much to the amusement of onlookers everywhere ... (Courtesy Paul Guinness)

Owners of the new roadster and roadster-coupé models launched in 2003 were quick to catch on to the modified scene, with enhanced versions of both appearing on the roads with impressive speed.

This particular example had front and rear panels and tridion safety cell colour-coordinated to match its original shine yellow paintwork. While the end result might not have appealed to those enthusiasts who liked the roadster's original colour contrasts, it certainly gave this example a unique and eye-catching look. (Courtesy Paul Guinness)

Modifying any smart roadster is all about knowing what you want to achieve and having a specific plan in mind. This example had its looks transformed thanks to an expensive respray in Rage Extreme Ecstasy, complemented by a set of BBS alloys, Eibach lowered (by 30mm) suspension and a restyled rear valance. The end result looked impressive from any angle.

Under the bonnet, meanwhile, a full remap combined with a K&N air filter and stainless steel high-performance exhaust system created a roadster with a useful 108bhp at its disposal. Who says a modified smart has to be all show and no go? (Courtesy Paul Guinness)

No prizes for guessing which country the owner of this 2002-model smart city-coupé calls home! The owner in question is Ian Dolphin, a British patriot who couldn't resist adorning his much-loved smart with his country's Union flag. Does he ever get embarrassed by all the attention it generates? Apparently not. "It does stand out from the crowd, I must admit," he says with a grin.

Apart from a set of eye-catching, seven-spoke alloys, a smarts-R-us engine remap, a K&N air filter and, of course, those fantastically eccentric body panels, Ian's city-coupé is fairly standard ... (Courtesy Paul Guinness)

Commercial buyers have always been aware of the smart's potential as a publicity vehicle – which helps explain why, in just about every market smart has entered, it has received a good proportion of business sales. And that's something very few other city cars can boast ... In this instance, here's a smart being used to promote a Norwegian nightclub, but wherever you go (particularly throughout Europe), you'll find smart's combination of head-turning style and cut-through-traffic driving characteristics winning it friends in the business world. From pizza companies to estate agents, city-based businesses have been won over by the charms of smart. (Courtesy Paul Guinness)

How cool is this? Back in 2006, Stefan Attart (Greek 4x4 Rally Champion) joined forces with Mercedes-Benz Greece to design and develop this amazing creation: a smart fortwo mounted on the chassis and running gear of the invincible Unimog 406-series truck. Known as the forfun^2, this incredible beast featured the Unimog's 5675cc, six-cylinder diesel engine, capable of producing a seriously massive amount of torque. Not only that, the forfun^2 offered ground clearance of more than two feet, off-road tyres on 26-inch rims, and an overall height of an astonishing twelve feet. The world's most outrageous smart? Probably. (Courtesy smart)

If you thought the smart fortwo couldn't get any smaller, think again. In fact, your local smart centre will happily supply you with a fortwo in miniature, a radio-controlled model that's guaranteed to offer endless fun to smart fans of all ages.

Model car maker Maisto also offers a 1:18 scale model of the fortwo, while Revell's 1:24 scale version of the fortwo has also won many fans. Whether you're doing an online search or paying a visit to your local model shop, you should have no difficulty finding a scaled-down smart to suit your budget. (Courtesy Paul Guinness)

chapter 6

the next generation

As popular as the original smart fortwo was (and, let's face it, sales of more than three quarters of a million in its first eight years of life was far better than many pundits predicted way back in 1998), it couldn't last forever without a complete redesign. It wasn't that there was anything intrinsically wrong with the fortwo; it's just that the city car market had moved on apace during those years.

And so, in April 2007, an all-new fortwo finally went on sale throughout much of Europe, arriving in the UK in right-hand drive form five months later and – crucially – destined for American sales (something that had so far eluded smart) from early 2008. It was this latter fact that made the redesign all the more important.

The small-car scene of the 21st century was drastically different from that of the late nineties. If the smart fortwo was to continue to attract buyers, it had to compete against well-designed European four-seater rivals like the Citroën C1. Furthermore, if it really was to go on sale in the USA after several years of rumour, even more changes would be necessary. There was no doubt about it, a brand new fortwo was the only way forward.

bigger and better

To describe the new-for-2007 fortwo as bigger than the original wouldn't be inaccurate, but would, perhaps, give the wrong impression. Maybe 'slightly less small' would be a better description, for the newcomer actually grew 195mm in length, of which just 55mm was dedicated to the wheelbase. This meant slightly larger front and rear overhangs than before, essential to enable the newcomer to meet European pedestrian crash safety regulations at the front, and American rear impact standards at the back.

There were plenty of changes under the skin, too, with the original smart-built turbocharged engine being replaced (on petrol-engined versions) by a Mitsubishi design – still with three cylinders but now a larger (999cc) capacity. While all smarts had previously featured a turbo, this was initially limited only to the most powerful (84bhp) version of the fortwo passion, with the standard 61 and 71bhp derivatives of the fortwo being normally-aspirated.

The original's six-speed sequential-style automatic transmission was also replaced, this time with a smoother-changing five-speed Getrag design that helped to make the whole driving experience that bit more relaxing. The smart fortwo, it seemed, was growing up.

The early years of the 21st century were financially tough for smart, with the company running up large losses, despite the popularity of most of its products. Owner Mercedes-Benz contemplated selling or closing the smart operation altogether at one point, but opted instead for rationalisation – which inevitably meant the end of the road for all but its core model, the fortwo. Even so, the original fortwo couldn't last forever – but how do you go about replacing such a unique and iconic concept? Designers were faced with a difficult balancing act. (Courtesy smart)

going green

Out on the road too, the all-new fortwo was a major improvement, with livelier performance, quicker steering, enhanced handling and better braking all contributing to a far more sophisticated feel. Happily though, the newcomer had lost none of its fun appeal, the fortwo remaining a highly manoeuvrable and entertaining little device in urban conditions – but now better than ever out on the open road.

Not surprisingly, Mercedes-Benz had high hopes for its latest smart fortwo, for it represented an important step forward – despite being no more expensive to buy than the model it replaced. But much of that optimism came about because of shifting priorities for car buyers throughout the world, with fuel consumption and reduced CO_2 emissions being increasingly important to

Destined for launch in 2007, the slightly bigger but still instantly recognisable all-new smart fortwo underwent months of intensive testing in some of the world's most inhospitable climates – and it wasn't long before photographs of disguised smarts under test began appearing in the motoring press.
No amount of disguise, however, could hide what smart fans everywhere had been hoping for: the proportions and the overall look that had made the original fortwo so unique in the first place were both still in place. The new fortwo would be a smart through and through. (Courtesy smart)

consumers by the time the fortwo finally went on sale in the USA in 2008. The smart fortwo had always been an ecologically viable machine – but buyers everywhere were now sitting up and taking notice.

Not only was the fortwo now more useable, more refined, more sophisticated and more practical than ever before, it was also one of the 'greenest' cars on sale anywhere, with normally-aspirated versions boasting an official CO2 emissions figure of just 112g/km – while the diesel model (still using the original smart diesel engine) did even better. By any standards, these were environmentally friendly machines.

There was no doubt about it: smart had entered a crucial new phase in its development. Thanks to much pre-launch

Wherever pre-production examples of the all-new fortwo went in the world, they were greeted by curious onlookers – but nowhere more so than in the USA, a market that smart was determined to crack with its newcomer.

Many of those Americans who caught sight of smart prototypes in disguise were shocked that a European car as small as the fortwo could ever go on sale in the USA. But with the cost of fuel at an all-time high, and concerns over CO2 emissions finally starting to affect people's buying habits, they could also see the logic of the diminutive smart. (Courtesy smart)

publicity in the USA, the future was looking rosy once more. At last, the smart fortwo could claim to be a genuinely global product.

On sale in Europe in 2007 and in the USA the following year, there was no mistaking the all-new fortwo (shown on the right) as anything other than a smart. Marginally bigger than its predecessor, smart's latest model was more sophisticated, more refined and more powerful, the latter thanks to its ex-Mitsubishi, 999cc three-cylinder engine.

Build costs for the newcomer were also significantly reduced, despite smart claiming a higher level of quality throughout. At last, it looked as though the popular little fortwo was about to start turning a profit for Mercedes-Benz. (Courtesy smart)

Right: Extra sales gave improved economies of scale, which meant smart could finally become profitable for Mercedes-Benz. And the best way to achieve this was by launching the all-new smart fortwo in the USA. What better mode of urban transport could there be for those congested city streets? Nothing was as easy to park or as economical to run as a fortwo, and smart made sure its publicity machine was up and running more than a year before the model's official American launch. By the summer of 2007, more than 20,000 potential buyers had taken advantage of smart's $99 car reservation offer. (Courtesy smart)

It's from this angle that the changes were most obvious between the old (left) and new fortwo models, with the latter's slight increase in length being evident both front and rear. European emphasis on pedestrian safety led to the marginally lengthened frontal look, while American rules regarding rear-end impact led to the strengthened and redesigned back. And yet, despite such design pressures, this was still unmistakably a smart fortwo: the same basic look, the same proportions, the same style and the same all-round cheekiness. The designers at smart had managed to pull off a rather clever trick. (Courtesy smart)

As before, the new fortwo was available in both coupé and cabrio guises, the latter combining the smart's unrivalled urban advantages with real wind-in-your-hair fun behind the wheel. While smart as a brand has never aimed to offer the cheapest city cars on the market (the fortwo has always been about innovation and aspiration rather than taking the cheap-and-cheerful approach), the cabrio continued the company's tradition of being the most affordable real convertible in most of the markets it entered. For those who wanted fresh-air motoring in a tiny package, the new fortwo cabrio took some beating. (Courtesy smart)

When smart announced its latest fortwo to the world's press in 2007, it was keen to stress that none of the company's original ideas had been lost, despite this being an all-new car: "The design has been skillfully further developed and gives the new smart fortwo a fresh, more masculine appearance. And yet it retains its unmistakable character: you can always tell a smart fortwo at first sight – by its striking tridion safety cell that is also one of the main safety features, and by the innovative plastic body panels that are extremely practical into the bargain." (Courtesy smart)

A smart just wouldn't be a smart without the company's innovative tridion safety cell, the impressively strong 'skeleton' from which the fortwo's plastic body panels were hung. As before, not only did this result in a city car with impressive integral strength, it also provided the fortwo with a distinct look – as well as giving buyers an opportunity to change body panels (and therefore the colour of their car) with amazing ease. Ulrich Walker, president of smart in 2007, said simply: "An excellent idea doesn't need to be reinvented." (Courtesy smart)

The new powerplant for the 2007-on fortwo was described by smart as a "state-of-the-art compact three-cylinder engine", and with plenty of justification. Power outputs of 61-84bhp were healthy for an engine of less than 1.0-litre capacity, while economy and CO2 emissions figures were also impressively competitive. The engine, designed and produced by Mitsubishi in Japan, was mounted transversely just in front of the rear axle, slanted at an angle of 45 degrees towards the rear. Britain's *Car* magazine said: "The Mitsu motors keep the mad three-pot thrum but deliver more torque and less thrash." (Courtesy smart)

With its bigger engine and extra power, even the 61bhp entry-level version of the smart fortwo – badged as the pure – felt lively out on the road. Inevitably, though, it was the 71bhp and 84bhp versions further up the range that offered the best combination of acceleration and cruising abilities.

When it came to cornering, the latest smart was also a major improvement, with even America's *Road & Track* magazine impressed after driving the newcomer in 2007: "Out on the road, the fortwo actually handles pretty well. The steering is direct and it's plenty fun to throw the car into a corner, with decent stability." (Courtesy smart)

Compared with the previous city-coupé and fortwo models, the latest offering from smart boasted more than enough boot space for most buyers' needs. In fact, if you were determined to fill the area behind the two seats to the roof with paraphernalia, you'd find up to 340 litres of space at your disposal. When its testers first took to the wheel of the 2007-on fortwo, Britain's *Car* magazine insisted "you'll be very surprised at how much a smart will swallow". And it was right; what this miniature marvel lacked in seating capacity, it more than made up for in load area. (Courtesy smart)

The interior of the all-new fortwo was a drastic departure from what had gone before. Where the original smarts had boasted quirky, idiosyncratic and daringly curvaceous dashboard designs, the newcomer's straight-across setup seemed a tad restrained by comparison. Sadly, though, it was an essential change if the smart fortwo was to comply with all current and future crash-test legislation, particularly in the crucial American market. In any case, smart's bold use of colours and its trademark eyes-on-stalks clock and rev counter mounted atop the dashboard helped inject a certain amount of character ... (Courtesy smart)

In every market the new fortwo entered, road testers praised smart for improving so much on its original concept – coming up with a car that was just as chic as before, but now much more developed in terms of both design and driving style. Britain's *Autocar* magazine wasn't afraid to praise smart's latest launch: "There's usefully more cabin and boot space in this evolved smart (the boot's now bigger than that of a Mini), plus discreet styling changes give the car a squarer-jawed, more masculine look." And it wasn't alone in its praise. (Courtesy smart)

The original smart city-coupé of 1998 was created as a modern, practical and desirable answer to the problems of urban transport. And a decade later, the concept was as relevant as ever, coupled with the buying public's desire for more eco-friendly cars in an effort to reduce carbon footprints. So, was the city-coupé ten years ahead of its time? Quite possibly. But the launch of the all-new fortwo in 2007 showed smart was more determined than ever to provide the ultimate in personal transport for city dwellers and commuters alike. The timing was suddenly perfect. (Courtesy smart)

If the original BMC Mini of the 1960s was the first economy car to cross class and income boundaries, smart was hoping the latest fortwo would achieve the same in the 21st century: "A smart is classless, it conveys a positive attitude to life. Its owner makes a statement: this is a well-informed person with a modern way of thinking and a sense of responsibility. The smart fortwo demonstrates the form that perfect urban mobility takes today. It is an automotive declaration of independence to the effect that this is all the car a person needs in the city." (Courtesy smart)

As with the previous fortwo, it didn't take long for those tuning specialists at BRABUS to get their hands on the all-new model announced in 2007, with the first examples of the latest BRABUS fortwo being shown to the public at that year's European motor shows. With various tweaks to the ex-Mitsubishi turbocharged engine, the new BRABUS had power boosted to 98bhp, which meant a new top speed of 95mph and – even more crucially – acceleration to match, with 0-62mph (100km/h) in a new low of just 9.9 seconds. The urban commute had never been so much fun ... (Courtesy smart)

CHAPTER 7

changing world

The long-awaited American debut of the latest fortwo in January 2008 couldn't have come at a better time for smart. It was, of course, significant that this – the 37th country in which smart was officially represented – was the biggest world market the company had ever entered. More importantly, though, the US-spec fortwo arrived at a time of rocketing fuel prices and major downsizing by large numbers of American new-car buyers.

With the benefit of hindsight, it was, perhaps, fortuitous for smart that it hadn't gone to America any earlier, for by 2008 the super-economical fortwo stood a far greater chance of success than at any other time in the marque's short history. Just as American motorists were becoming concerned about the cost of fuel and the environmental impact of running large-engined machines, along came the smart fortwo – the answer to many a city dweller's prayers.

The fortwo had, of course, been cleverly marketed and hyped long before its official on-sale date, giving prospective buyers a chance to order a car and 'build' its specification online during 2007. So it's little wonder that the fortwo got off to a flying start in the USA in January '08, with more than 11,000 examples delivered to their new owners by the middle of the year.

It's also significant that smart chose to launch the US-spec fortwo during the marque's tenth anniversary year, at a time when the company's future looked particularly healthy. While other car manufacturers began experiencing plummeting sales in many of their main export markets, caused by the global credit crunch and impending recession, smart's fortwo suddenly held huge appeal for large numbers of economy-conscious buyers.

With sales increasing and smart also looking towards China as its next major export market, the marque's tenth anniversary was something well worth celebrating. But smart couldn't afford to be complacent, with rival manufacturers determined to get involved in the city car scene – including Toyota with its innovative iQ. And so, determined to stay ahead of the game, smart announced variations in such areas as electric drive and stop-start technology, paving the way for future upgrades for the fortwo – renowned as one of the 'greenest' new-car choices on the planet.

The motoring world faced uncertain times, massively affected by the global economic downturn. But smart continued to enjoy increased sales, producing exactly the right product at exactly the right time. The new generation fortwo was the success it genuinely deserved to be.

Despite more manufacturers entering the city car market, smart continued to prosper with its second generation fortwo, with increased sales during 2008. In the UK, in particular, the latest fortwo was finding new fans, with more than 7000 cars sold during the year – a 44 per cent increase on 2007. The previous generation, diesel-engined fortwo cdi had never been sold in Britain, but smart announced that a right-hand drive version of the latest cdi would be heading to the UK from February 2009 – finally giving British customers a chance to enjoy the vehicle with the lowest CO2 emissions of any production car at just 88g/km. (Courtesy smart)

While the smart fortwo was never going to head the Top Ten best-sellers list in America, it didn't take long for the cute two-seater to establish its own niche, aided by a new trend for downsizing by many urban-based American buyers. In fact, once smart had convinced prospective buyers that the fortwo could be just as safe, just as stable and even roomier (for two) than a conventional car, American buyers with imagination wasted no time in ordering their new smarts. More than 11,000 fortwos were sold in the USA during the model's first six months, far more than many pundits had predicted. (Courtesy smart)

Little more than a year on from the launch of the second generation fortwo, the company would be celebrating the tenth anniversary of the very first smart car rolling off the production line at Hambach, France – back in July 1998. And in that time, more than 900,000 cars had been produced in total, putting smart within easy reach of achieving its one-millionth sale. The product had changed a lot over those ten years, the latest version being slightly larger, more powerful, more economical, less polluting and more spacious than what had gone before. The latest smart was a revelation. (Courtesy smart)

If the world's major cities were to tackle issues of overcrowding, they had to rethink the whole concept of personal transport, suggested smart in 2008. And so the German city of Ulm – together with smart – launched its car2go scheme, comprising a fleet of fortwos that would act as pool cars, providing economical, reliable transport within the city limit for 19 cents (€0.19) per minute.
Once registered with car2go, a customer's driving licence was provided with an electronic chip that enabled the car to be unlocked, allowing users to make use of a smart fortwo wherever they found one in Ulm – a brilliantly simple idea! (Courtesy smart)

With the second generation fortwo, smart went to great lengths to ensure it was even safer than the previous model, essential if such a minuscule machine was to be sold in the USA. So, nobody could blame smart for shouting about its achievements – the pinnacle of which was its British TV advertising campaign of 2008. This particular advert showed a one tonne wrecking ball smashing into a new fortwo at 25mph (40km/h), the stunt actor emerging with a smile from a remarkably unscathed car. As a powerful portrayal of toughness and safety, it was beyond compare. (Courtesy smart)

Many people who had never sat in a smart, even ten years on from the launch of the original model, took some convincing that this was a roomy car. So, not only did smart UK release a TV advert showing the latest fortwo being loaded with a washing machine, it also arranged a few live stunts – including this, at the 2008 smart Destination Brooklands event. The idea was to see how many contortionists could be crammed into a new fortwo. The answer? An astonishing thirteen, going by the group name of the 'smart car-tortionists.' Just don't try this at home ... (Courtesy smart)

It was an open secret that smart would be releasing an all-electric version of the fortwo in 2010, but the company had to make sure the product was well developed, reliable, and exactly what electric car buyers were looking for. So, as early as 2008, the company released 100 pre-production fortwo ed (electric drive) vehicles for trials in hard-working situations – including a pair on loan to London's Metropolitan Police. Ideal for urban situations, the zero-emissions fortwo ed boasted a claimed top speed of 60mph (97km/h), nought to 30mph (48km/h) in 6.5 seconds, and a range of up to 70 miles (113km) between charges. (Courtesy smart)

The previous fortwo had been the subject of various special editions over the years, and smart wasted no time in following suit with the second generation model in the summer of 2008 – with the launch of the aptly-named limited two. Based around the 71bhp fortwo passion and available in coupé or cabrio guises, the limited two boasted a unique light blue metallic paint finish that 'altered' its shade according to the light, as well as these rather striking brown leather heated seats. Special badging and six-spoke alloys were also part of the impressive package, which, in the UK, cost from £9575. (Courtesy smart)

Happy 10th birthday, smart! After going through some turbulent times, smart was determined to mark its tenth anniversary in July 2008. It had been a decade of highs and lows, successes and failures. But, by the time the first ten years had passed, smart's future was looking assured once again – largely thanks to the success of the latest fortwo and its expansion into new territory. In fact, the fortwo was suddenly the car that recession-hit buyers were looking for, particularly in an era of soaring fuel prices. As Dr Dieter Zetsche, head of Mercedes-Benz, said of the fortwo: "Had we not invented it ten years ago, we would have to do so now." (Courtesy smart)

Keen to retain its reputation as the greenest car manufacturer on the planet, smart introduced micro hybrid drive (mhd) to 61bhp and 71bhp versions of the latest fortwo towards the end of 2008, providing as standard a stop-start function to improve fuel economy and lower emissions still further. In fact, smart was claiming fuel savings of up to 24 per cent, combined with CO_2 emissions as low as just 103g/km. Also part of the new 2009 specification were redesigned instruments with enhanced LCD display, net storage pockets in the doors, new colour choices, and the option of 15-inch, six-spoke alloys. (Courtesy smart)

The LCD display says 'ECO' – and that just about sums up the micro hybrid drive (mhd) feature of the 2009 fortwo models. The mhd system operated during engine idling phases (ideal for the urban driving of most smart owners), the engine stopping when the setup sensed that the smart's speed had dropped below 5mph and the driver was braking. When the driver released the brake pedal, the engine restarted automatically. The stop-start facility operated seamlessly, largely thanks to the powerful belt-driven starter generator that replaced both the conventional starter and alternator, and made no extra demands on the driver. (Courtesy smart)

With the much-hyped American launch of the fortwo safely out of the way, it was time for smart to turn its attention to the world's biggest emerging car market: China. After exhibiting the fortwo at the Auto China show of 2008, smart announced that official Chinese sales would get under way by mid-2009. Inevitably, the fortwo would be marketed there as a premium product, with high import taxes making it impossible to compete on price with home-built economy cars. But that didn't stop Dr Dieter Zetsche, head of Mercedes-Benz, from remaining optimistic: "I am sure that many lifestyle-oriented customers in China's cities will soon come to love its concept." (Courtesy smart)

More than a decade on from the debut of the original city-coupé, the latest smart fortwo continues the good work, establishing the brand in new markets and building on its success elsewhere. Who could have predicted in 1998 that American buyers would be taking this innovative city car to their hearts? The fact is, the world is changing, with car buyers now having different priorities and demands, and the smart fortwo giving increasing numbers of these buyers exactly what they want. The city car brand that Mercedes-Benz came so close to killing off during its darkest days is now seen as a valuable asset with an invaluable product. (Courtesy smart)

Looking ahead now, at the end of the first decade of the 21st century, what does the future hold for smart? Expectations are vastly different from those of earlier days, when smart planned a four-model range – including an SUV – in order to crack America and be a success. These days, the emphasis is purely and simply on the fortwo – a car that offers style, economy, low emissions, practicality, and fashion status in one tiny package. But what will the next generation fortwo look like? Only time will tell, though you can be sure of one thing: smart's ability to innovate and surprise is here to stay. (Courtesy smart)

the family smart

It was an open secret that the management at smart wanted to see this impressively youthful car brand expand into new markets as soon as possible, which helps explain why the roadster and roadster-coupé were both launched just five years after the very first city-coupé. What smart really needed to boost sales, though, was a four-seater hatchback capable of competing with Europe's top superminis. Or so smart thought.

In reality, the new smart forfour of 2004 – created in conjunction with Mitsubishi and produced alongside the latter's Colt model in The Netherlands – turned out to be a total failure, with sales falling well below expectations: the decision was made within just a few months of its launch that the car simply couldn't survive.

The smart forfour was a decent design, and offered a genuinely different alternative to the BMW-owned MINI of the time. It also looked like a smart (thanks to its tridion design, naturally), offered plenty of interior innovation and was a genuinely fine drive. But, quite simply, it wasn't what smart buyers wanted – and by 2006, it was dead. A sad end for one of the few genuinely interesting hatchbacks of the time ...

Work began on designing the new family smart – but exactly which direction should it go in? In terms of concept, there was really only one option: the newcomer had to use the existing and instantly recognisable tridion safety cell idea if it was to be a 'proper' smart. It was such an important part of the company's brand values and identity that to have a non-tridion smart in the line-up would have been unthinkable. But what should the newcomer look like? Various design proposals were put forward before smart's final decision on the forfour was made. (Courtesy smart)

It was an open secret that the new smart forfour was being developed in conjunction with Mitsubishi. And that's why the new-for-2004 Mitsubishi Colt shared many of its underpinnings with the smart. It saved both companies a not-so-small fortune in development costs, and enabled them to share production facilities at Mitsubishi's Dutch plant.

It was a relationship that benefited both concerns, even if the forfour ended up being one of the shortest-lived models of recent years – thanks to both disappointing sales and a realisation on the part of smart owner Mercedes-Benz that drastic action was called for. (Courtesy smart)

It wasn't just the tridion that gave the smart forfour its unique appearance. With its quad ovoid headlamps set into the front panel, broad-grinned front grille, steeply sloped windscreen set well forward and seriously flared wheelarches, the entire design boasted a squat, masculine and sporty look. In fact, the forfour was one of the most individualistic five-door hatchbacks of its generation, and all achieved without employing any of the 'retro cuteness' that designers of the MINI and the New Beetle had already made full use of. The forfour was like nothing else in its class. (Courtesy smart)

So who would be buying the new forfour? The simple answer (with the benefit of hindsight) is: not enough people. But back at the time of the forfour's launch, smart was suggesting it could appeal to the kind of buyer who would otherwise opt for a MINI or Volkswagen's New Beetle. The existence of both models proved there was a market for modern hatchbacks with more than a touch of individuality – so how could the forfour possibly fail? Fail, though, it did. Despite favourable press reviews at the time, the forfour simply didn't sell strongly enough to justify keeping it in production. (Courtesy smart)

The interior of the forfour engendered almost as many headlines as its external styling – and the most talked about feature was what smart referred to as "the ingenious new lounge concept", providing maximum versatility inside.
The back rests of the two front seats, for example, could be folded down so they were almost level with the rears to create a large horizontal seat surface – ideal for 'chilling out' or when parked up for a rest. The rear seat bench could also be adjusted by 150 millimetres in length, while rotatable arm rests ensured you'd always find a relaxing position. (Courtesy smart)

It was always the intention that smart would offer a four-car range by 2006, comprising the fortwo, forfour, roadster – and this, the company's planned SUV. To be known as the formore, this all-important 4x4 was to be the vehicle that finally catapulted smart into the American market. However, following the decision to cease production of both the roadster and forfour ranges as part of smart's cost-cutting strategy, the entire formore project was also canned. It was a great shame, because a compact SUV oozing unmistakable smart style could have succeeded – but Mercedes-Benz was taking no chances. From now on, smart would be concentrating on what it did best: producing clever, innovative and desirable two-seater city cars.

Petrol engine choices for the new forfour were restricted to a 1124cc (74bhp) six-valve, three-cylinder unit or – for those who preferred more conventional powerplants – 1332cc and 1449cc eight-valve, four-cylinder lumps, the latter developing 95 and 107bhp respectively. Performance was excellent by class standards, with the 1.3 boasting a top speed of 111mph, and the 1.5 managing 118mph flat-out. With handling and roadholding (not to mention impressively sharp steering) to match, the driving experience was surprisingly good fun. Diesel choice was confined to a 1.5-litre, three-cylinder turbo, designed by Mercedes-Benz and available in 68 or 95bhp states of tune. (Courtesy smart)

smart online

To find out more about the smart fortwo in any of the countries in which it is currently represented, either use the direct links below or log on to www.smart.com and select your country of choice. You will then be redirected to the company's official website specific to your market.

USA – www.smartusa.com

EUROPE – www.smart.com

CANADA – www.thesmart.ca

AUSTRALIA – www.smartaustralia.com.au

SOUTH AFRICA – www.smart.co.za

JAPAN – www.smart-j.com

individual 1

MICROCARS AT LARGE!

Adam Quellin

An entertaining and informative insight into the world of some of the most unusual and obscure promotional vehicles from around the globe. Lavishly illustrated with colour and black and white photographs of cars, vans and trucks spanning a hundred year period, this collection of oddball vehicles is guaranteed to raise a smile.
ISBN 978-1-845840-03-7
£12.99*

An extensively illustrated reference guide to classic scooters and microcars with specification data presented in A-Z order. Nostalgic recollections by the author based on ownership and personal experience bring to life these facinating vehicles.
ISBN 978-1-845840-88-4
£14.99*

THE WONDERFUL WACKY WORLD OF MARKETINGMOBILES

PROMOTIONAL VEHICLES OF THE WORLD

JAMES HALE

index